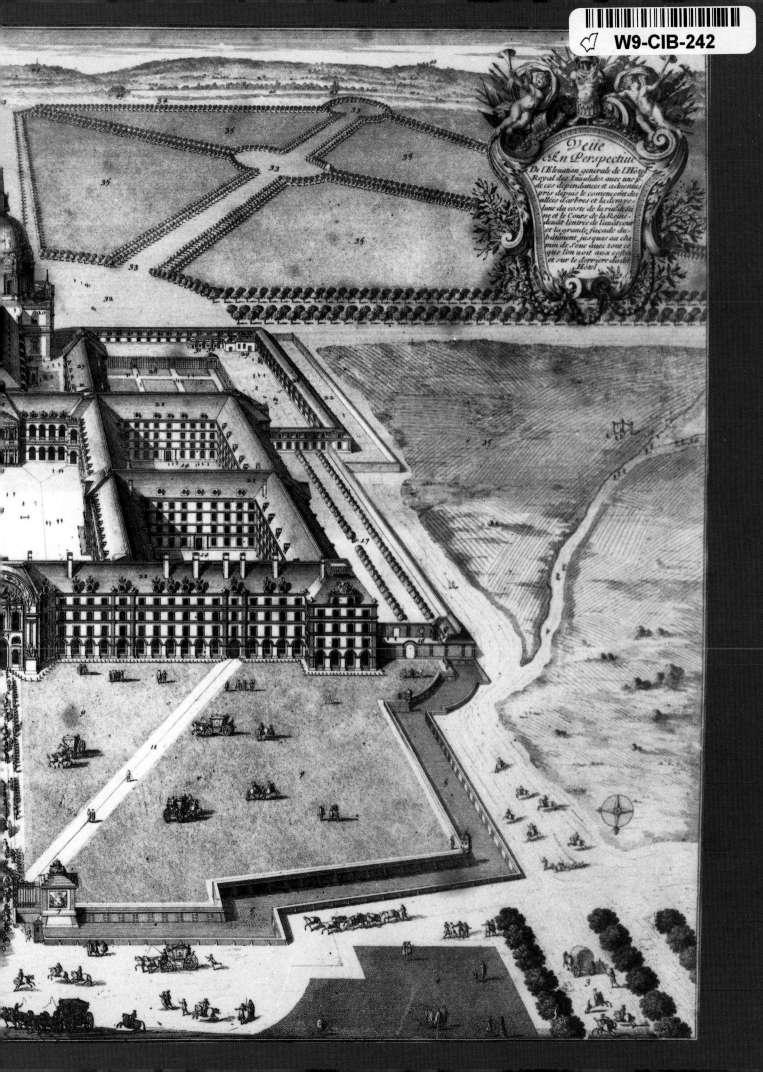

Veüe
En Perspectiue
De l'Eleuation generale de l'Hôtel
Royal des Inualides, auec une p.
de ces dependances et aduenües
pris depuis le comencent des
allées d'arbres et la demye-
luë du coste de la riuadefi-
ne et le Cours de la Reine
deuât l'entre de laud cour
et la grande façade du
bâtiment jusques au che-
mun de Seue auec tout ce
que l'on uoit aux costés
et sur le derriere dudit
Hôtel

Cover: aerial view of
the Hôtel des Invalides.
© Y. Arthus-
Bertrand/Altitude

pages 2-3 and 66-67:
Pierre Lepautre,
General view of the
Hôtel royal des

Invalides, engraving
from Description
générale de l'Hostel
royal des Invalides,
by Le Jeune de
Boulencourt, 1683.
© Musée de
l'Armée, Paris.

Above: Charles Le
Brun, Allegory of the
construction of the
Hôtel des Invalides,
ceiling painting
in the Mirror Gallery
at Versailles.
© Giraudon.

THE INVALIDES
AND THE ARMY MUSEUM

CONTENTS

THE HISTORY OF THE INVALIDES

"Day and night, people steal and kill here and around Paris... We have reached the dregs of all the centuries" complained the disputatious doctor Gui Patin. Boileau went further, saying "Paris is less safe than the most gloomy wood", and he avoided venturing onto the Pont-Neuf, the meeting point of a rather doubtful crowd: tooth-pullers, fortune-tellers, cut-purses, idlers and beggars of all descriptions, not to mention, in this court of miracles, the old disabled soldiers, homeless and unable to assure their own upkeep.

Ever since the signing of the Peace of the Pyrenees in 1659, Louis XIV had never ceased to dream of founding an institution for the care of the severely wounded and the lodging of old soldiers. The idea was not new, but the many projects devised before his time under the reigns of Henri III, Henri IV and Louis XIII had never materialized. Failing anything better, a hybrid solution had been arrived at: the right of oblate, which imposed on certain abbeys the upkeep of an old soldier who was incapable, infirm or impoverished. This lay-person chosen by royal prerogative received the name of oblate or lay-monk. However, this measure satisfied no-one, for the disabled veterans were hardly old men steeped in piety. Unable to follow monastic rules, they were for the most part undesirables in the eyes of the abbots, who most often tried to escape this commitment.

Tired of all this confusion, Louis XIV, who had ordered a census of all the priories and abbeys that received lay-monks, finally revealed his grand plan in an ordinance dated 24 February 1670: the monarch cut short all the havering and announced the setting up of a public building to provide shelter for the old age of his soldiers. It was to be built in Paris, at one end of the faubourg Saint Germain. Several ordinances followed, fixing Louis XIV's aims which he confirmed in the edict that established the building: "...to construct a royal building of sufficient size and space to receive and lodge all officers and men who are crippled or old and frail and to guarantee sufficient funds for their subsistance and their upkeep." While the royal building was being constructed, the first invalids were housed, from 1 October 1670, in

the heart of the faubourg Saint-Germain, in a large mansion rented from the Sieur d'Herval in the rue Cherche-Midi, at the cross-roads with Croix-Rouge. At the same time, Louvois, Louis XIV's war minister, who was in charge of carrying out the royal plan, had the land of the Grenelle plain purchased, situated between the Sèvres road (the current rue de Sèvres) and the Seine. It was Louis XIV himself who chose, from among the eight projects presented to him, that of Libéral Bruant, a 36 year old architect who had just completed the construction of the Salpêtrière almshouse. For the future building, Bruant proposed a grid plan over a ten hectare area. As soon as the first stone was laid, on 30 November 1671, Louvois and his administrators, the three Camus brothers, personally kept a close watch on the smooth running of the building works, constantly bullying the contractors, clambering up the scaffolding and demanding the instant dismissal of any worker they deemed incompetent.

In October 1674, the band of invalids entered into their palace to the sound of fifes and drums. They were received by Louis XIV in person, accompanied by Louvois and the hospice's governor, François Lemaçon d'Ormoy. The old soldiers, mostly survivors of the Thirty Years War, were moved to tears, and brought the house down with their cheers. Their years of misery forgotten, their old days were definitively assured thanks to the benevolence of the Sun King.
But the building was far from terminated as the church had still to be built. This had to assume the double function of

church for the king and church for the soldiers. Libéral Bruant had an unsteady grasp of the project. His designs stagnated, he wasted time... In short he hesitated so much that he annoyed Louvois, who was little inclined to be in any way indulgent towards a client of his rival Colbert! Finally, in March 1676, Louvois summoned a young 30 year old architect to the site: Jules Hardouin-Mansart. Three weeks later, this great-nephew of the celebrated Mansart sent his plans to Louvois, who, while expressing a few minor criticisms, recognised that the young architect had solved the problem of protocol that had been a stumbling-block for Libéral Bruant. The king and his ministers therefore accepted the project and work started again.

Thirty years later, on 28 August 1706, in the dôme courtyard, 600 invalids in battle formation received Louis XIV accompanied by the Dauphin, the dukes of Burgundy and Berry, the Queen and several princesses. His Majesty came to inaugurate the royal church, consecrated to Saint Louis. At the entrance, Hardouin-Mansart bowed before the king, saying: "Sire, I have the honour to present at your Majesty's feet the key of this sacred temple that your piety has caused to be raised for the glory of God. I shall be happy if this work that you have entrusted to my care for thirty years can respond to the high idea that Your Majesty has given me of it, and to his wise counsel! This superb monument to your faith will be a sign to the most distant posterity of the splendour of your reign."
The monarch was impressed by the scene within the church, resplendent in all its gold, all the more as he found that the

cupola painted by Lafosse had at last been completed. The definitive decoration was deployed in a skil-
ful balance of painting and sculpture: the painters
dealing with the celestial parts and the soaring lyri-
cism, the sculptors with the more down to earth level
of the building. For the first time, the Te Deum and
the Exaudiat lit up the grandiose vault, sung by four
choirs of more than 150 singers perched up in the
galleries. The congregation was subjugated and let
itself be carried away by the wave of emotion that
inundated the nave as the Cardinal de Noailles celebrated mass. These unforgettable moments sufficed
to reward the king for all his efforts. And yet, Louis
XIV had no idea it was to be his last visit to his che-
rished institution...

Ever since the Sun King had inaugurated the dome,
the Hôtel Royal des Invalides had become the Parisian's favourite promenade. While the classical
beauty of the site was being admired, the pensioners,
recognisable in their costumes of blue cloth, were
the object of the most lively solicitude. And visitors
posed a thousand questions to the old veterans about
their life in this veritable little town. The harmonious
cohabitation of more than a thousand men of all
ages, from all parts of the country, and of all ranks,
was a feat of prowess. The secret of the success of
Louis XIV and Louvois was to be found in the im-
position of military organisation in the institution.
Indeed the hospice ranked as a fortress, and the pensioners, organised in companies, had to obey the
rules of military drill as well as the demands of a religious foundation.

After a difficult start the success of the royal institution asserted itself; intended to house 1500 invalids,
those wishing to enter numbered nearly 6000 from
1676 to 1690. And when room was lacking, draco-
nian conditions of admission were imposed. Thus
ten years' minimum service was required for a soldier or trooper, a period that was even extended to

twenty years in 1710. Failing this, one had to be "absolutely incapable of serving, either because of extreme old age or frailty, or because of injury or incurable illness." It was the governor's responsability to control the records, to unmask the simulators and encroachers. Moreover the hospice was prohibited to patients with scrofula and to sailors, for whom Colbert had allocated pensions. Protestants, accepted up until the revocation of the edict of Nantes in 1685, were tolerated on condition of renouncing their religion. Despite their severity the rules did not prevent notes of request, some from the king, others from high-ranking military leaders, but most often signed by Louvois himself.

Once accepted, the candidate presented himself at the entrance gate of the hospice. As soon as he arrived at the control point for registration, he received a comb, a wooden spoon and a knife; the tailor took his measurements to make him a uniform, and a shoemaker took the form of his feet. Eight days later, he returned to the control point to receive his costume, a chamois jacket, a black hat, two pairs of grey stockings, body linen, shoes and the sacrosanct numbered card, a veritable passport within the hospice.

The new recruits were forthwith placed in the care of the priests and confined to the institution for a period of forty days, the duration of their religious instruction. Housing varied according to the rank of the pensioner. Officers slept two or three in a heated room; soldiers on the other hand were grouped in small dormitories of four or six beds. Though the invalids could circulate freely within the hospice they were not able to leave without authorisation from the governor. The rules prevented them from keeping wine and food in their rooms, much more so eating and drinking. Tobacco was banned and any trade within the hospice prohibited under pain of expulsion. Women were not allowed in, although married invalids were authorised to sleep out twice a week... This was not allowed on Saturdays, however, as all pensioners were obliged to attend Sunday mass! Any breach of discipline was severely dealt with and the range of punishments was in proportion to the nature of the offence: from being put on water rations to expulsion to the hospice at Bicêtre, not to mention public exposure on the wooden horse... Minutely regulated service at table set the day's rhythm. The officers met at 11.45 a.m. and 7 p.m. in rooms

Below, left to right:
from Boulay,
*le baron d'Espagnac
bestowing favour on
an invalid c. 1770,*
lithograph.
© Musée
de l'Armée, Paris.

Jean-Baptiste
Lallemand,
*Looting of weapons
in the Invalides
on the morning
of 14 July 1789,*
oil on canvas,
54 x 64 cm.
Musée
Carnavalet, Paris.
© Musées
de la Ville de Paris,
Spadem 1993.

specially reserved for them. They sat down in groups of twelve at round tables set out with tablecloths, napkins, pewter dishes and silver cutlery bearing the royal monogram. Sergeants and other ranks were assigned to four large refectories overlooking the eastern and western galleries of the royal courtyard. They dined and supped in two services: 11 and 11.45 a.m.; 6 and 6.45 p.m. Tablecloths, dishes and pewter cutlery were laid out on long wooden tables at which each pensioner had his alloted place.

Set out conspicuously in the centre of each refectory, which contained eight large tables, was the table for those drinking water. This was for the pensioners who had been punished; it was a way of causing remorse to those who had broken the rules or who had

From top to bottom and from left to right:
Jules Varnier, *Portrait of Jean-Mathieu Philibert Serurier,* (1742-1819), oil on canvas, 139 x 87 cm, present office of the Director of the Army Museum. © Musée de l'Armée, Paris.

Jean-Baptiste Debret, *First investiture of the Légion d'honneur in the Church of the Invalides on 15 July 1804,* 1812, 403 x 531 cm. Château de Versailles. © RMN.

Right-hand page: Alexandre Veron-Bellecourt, *Napoleon visiting the infirmary of the Invalides on 11 February 1808,* oil on canvas, 183 x 248 cm. Château de Versailles. © RMN.

a debt to pay off to the hospice... The blind, those with severe facial wounds and those with only one arm had their own refectory. For these men, incapable of feeding themselves, a permanent auxiliary service was financed by the institution.

In the area of hygiene the Hôtel Royal des Invalides broke new ground. Two lavatories with seats for the use of the soldiers were installed in the main building. With 300 individual beds, an exceptional luxury for the time, the nurses dispensed their treatment without distinction of rank. 37 grey sisters or daughters of Charity, aided by lay brothers, held sway over these premises from 6 March 1676, the date of the contract with Louvois. They even imposed their authority on the medical corps, which comprised a doctor, a surgeon and an apothecary. After six years of service in the hospice, the latter acquired full qualifications without any other form of examination and were subsequently able to practise freely in Paris.

For Louvois the worst enemy of the institution was idleness. He consequently incorporated the most able-bodied in the armed detachments that kept guard in frontier towns such as Dieppe, Lisieux, Honfleur, Saint Malo, Mézières or Doullens but also at the gates of the capital. The others worked in manufacturing workshops set up in the hospice. Uniforms were made, stockings, shoes, matches, and even finely woven tapestries in the purest Savonnerie style, and let us not forget to mention the finest

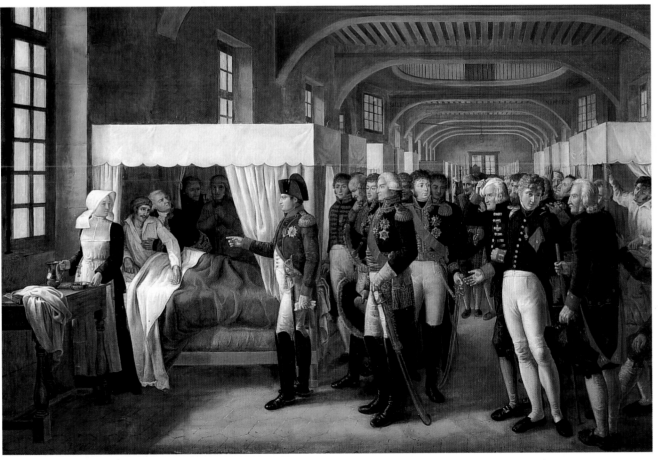

ornament of this activity: the workshop for calligraphy and illuminating which even worked for Versailles. The renown of the Hôtel Royal des Invalides rapidly went beyond the borders of the kingdom, becoming an inevitable stop for foreign sovereigns visiting Paris: the Elector of Bavaria, Leopold I, Tsar Peter the Great, the King of Denmark, Christian VII and by the future Gustav III of Sweden. The infirmaries, copied throughout all Europe, were to serve as the basis of the first military hospital that Louis XIV had dreamed of. And under the guidance of the senior surgeon a new school of anatomy and surgery was born. It was here, in 1791, that Dominique Larrey, the famous surgeon of the Grande Armée, made his début under the wing of the great Sabatier. And it was also in the Invalides that a certain Antoine-Augustin Parmentier, more famous for his work in connection with the potato, was apothecary. It is still possible to see the laboratory in which he started his research into the chemistry of nutrition.

Although the Revolution started in the Invalides on the morning of 14 July 1789 by the pillaging of the 32,000 guns stored in the cellars, the hopsice was able to resist the devastating onrush. At first threatened with disappearence in favour of "hospices of the fatherland", the institution survived despite everything. The only change concerned its name, the Constituent Assembly rebaptising it, on 30 April 1789, the "National hospice for military invalids". As was the case with other Parisian monuments the hospice

lost its royal emblems and the church was stripped of its religious attributes in order to turn it into a temple of Mars. It was in this frigid place that the brand new republic was to prostrate itself before the trophies conquered by its armies.

But the emergence of Napoleon quickly restored prestige to the venerable institution. The Emperor went back to Louis XIV's grand plan: he had the outrages of the Revolution effaced, returned the church to religious service, ordered the re-gilding of the dome, and by the organic decree of 25 March 1811, endowed the imperial institution with a budget paid for from military salaries in excess of 500 francs, from those of members of the Légion d'honneur and from various duties imposed on land rents, shipwrecks, salt works in the east etc. Napoleon also decided to make of the Invalides a necropolis, before distributing there the first stars of the Légion d'honneur on 15 July 1804. As it was the custom to bury the governors of the Invalides beneath the chancel of the soldiers' church, the Emperor chose the church under the dome for the reception of the body of Turenne in 1800 and the heart of Vauban eight years later.

The Restoration brought with it no upsets. The hospice of the Invalides remained the pantheon of military glory. On 15 December 1840 it received the ashes of Napoleon I at the end of a grandiose ceremony orchestrated by the July Monarchy and immortalised by Victor Hugo in

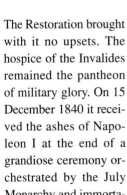

Choses vues. However another 21 years went by before the remains of the Emperor found their permanent resting-place in the monumental porphyry sarcophagus designed by the architect Visconti. Later the remains of Jérôme Bonaparte, King of Westphalia and also an ephemeral governor of the Invalides, were laid to rest there, as were those of his wife Princess Catherine of Wurtemberg and those of the King of Spain, Joseph Bonaparte.

Among the heroes of French military history feature La Tour d'Auvergne, the first grenadier of the Republic killed at Berhausen in 1800, Marshals Bugeaud, Lyautey, Foch and Leclerc. Even Rouget de Lisle, the author and composer of the Marseillaise, is buried there, but only by accident: in 1915 he was given temporary burial there awaiting transferal to the Pantheon, but this never took place. He was rejoined on 15 December

1992 by the surgeon of the Napoleonic era: after 150 years of purgatory in the Père Lachaise cemetery Larrey was at last laid to rest among his old soldiers and his Emperor, just as he had always wished. In the aftermath of the defeat of 1870 a new vocation devolved on the Invalides: whereas the hospice as an institution went into progressive decline (1052 pensioners in 1870, 488 in 1880) the building became a sanctuary for arms, receiving the exhibits of the Artillery Museum as early as 1871, then those of the Historical Army Museum in 1896. The two institutions were merged in 1905 to become the Army Museum. These collections consolidated an earlier museum founded by Louis XVI in the Invalides in 1776 with all the relief plans, those glories of Louis XIV's reign, at first deposited in the Tuileries, then in the Louvre, and over which a detached company of invalids kept guard night and day. Under the Third

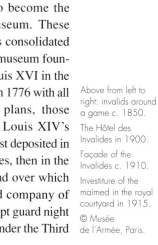

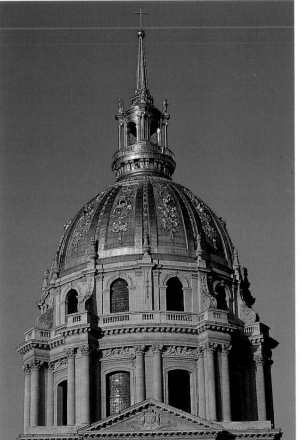

Republic new collections led to the expansion of the museum, alas too often at the expense of the invalid soldiers. Worse, Louis XIV's institution seemed condemned even despite World War I. Clémenceau himself doubted its utility. And yet, the hospice survived, and when the general mobilisation of September 1939 was announced about a hundred invalids were evacuated to their rest-home in Tessé-la-Madeleine, near Bagnoles-de-l'Orne. On 23 June 1940 the building received the most unexpected of visitors: Hitler came to meditate before Napoleon's tomb. That day he decided to return to France the ashes of l'Aiglon, Napoleon's son. The ceremony took place on the following 15 December at 1 a.m. In the freezing night air 200 republican guards from Paris formed a double line which stretched from the dome courtyard right up to the church. Drums were beating on the parade ground while German grenadiers

Below from left to right: restoration of the dome in 1937. © Musée de l'Armée, Paris.
The dome of the Invalides Church regilded in 1989. © JP Lescourret/ Explorer.

placed the bronze sarcophagus before the entrance gate. It was then carried to the high altar where the prince's coffin rested on a simple catafalque, veiled by an immense tricolore which draped down over the steps. The Invalides was to experience other unexpected adventures during the war. In 1942 a resistance network chose to settle at the foot of the dome. Under the noses of the Germans who were quartered in the building, an escape route was set up for British and American pilots shot down over Normandy. 130 pilots thus transited by the Invalides before the Gestapo discovered the organisation on 5 July 1944, only two months before the liberation of Paris.

Since then the Invalides has resumed its triple vocation of institution to receive veterans wounded in the service of their country, pantheon of military glory and guardian of the historical memory of France.

Anne Muratori-Philip

THE SOLDIERS PALACE

The Hôtel des Invalides is, after the château of Versailles, the most important architectural edifice of the reign of Louis XIV. Its modest purpose, far removed from the splendour of the royal palace, lent it a more discreet fame. Yet its royal church is one of the masterpieces of the national classicism that Jacques-François Blondel traced back to François Mansart, "the god of architecture".

In 1670 Louis XIV founded the Hôtel des Invalides, choosing the plan of Libéral Bruant. This new institution had a complex programme: part hospital, part hospice, part barracks, even part monastery for this "militia in heaven's service". The clarity of the plan effected a synthesis that borrowed from the Salpêtrière hospital, designed by Le Vau around 1660, and from the barracks that Louvois was to design. His gridded plan, contrary to what is usually supposed, probably owes nothing to the famous palace-monastery of the Escorial built a century earlier near Madrid, as it had become common practice in Jesuit hospitals or colleges. The absolute symmetry around a central axis, perpendicular to the Seine, gives

Aerial view of
the Invalides with the
esplanade and
the Pont Alexander III
in the background.
© Yann Arthus-
Bertrand/Altitude.

A dormer window
on the northern
façade
of the Invalides.
© A. Derenne/
La Goëlette.

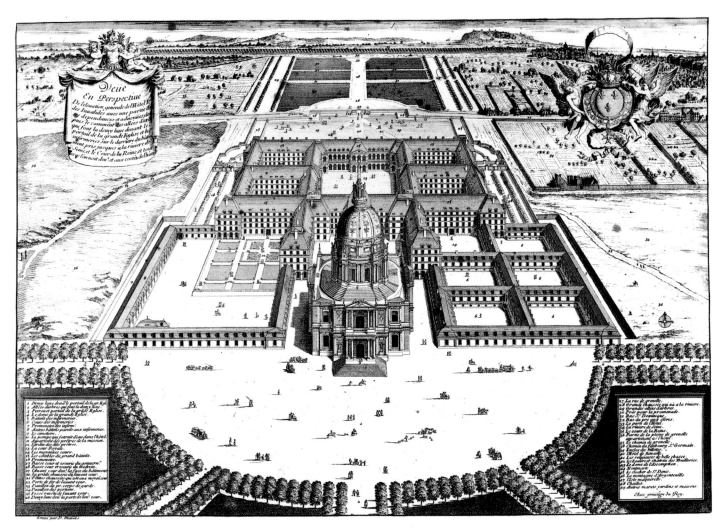

Above: view in
perspective of
the Hôtel National
des Invalides.
© Musée
de l'Armée, Paris.

Right:
*The King sets out for
the Netherlands
War*, engraving from
*Description
générale de l'Hostel
royal des Invalides*
by Le Jeune de
Boulencourt,

Paris, 1683.
© Musée
de l'Armée, Paris.

Right-hand page,
from top to bottom:
Félibien,
engraving from
*Description de
l'église royale des
Invalides*, 1706,
church square with
semi-circular
colonnade in front of
the Dome Church,
project not carried

out, c. 1680.
© Musée
de l'Armée, Paris.

Pierre-Denis Martin,
*Louis XIV visiting the
Hôtel royal
des Invalides on
26 August 1706*,
oil on canvas,
110 x 160 cm.
Musée Carnavalet,
Paris.
© Musées de la Ville
de Paris, Spadem
1993.

articulation to the esplanade, forecourt, central pavilion, royal courtyard and church. On the Seine side a vast esplanade, originally just a deserted plain, leads to the main building. Once through the entrance gate one finds oneself in a forecourt with on one side Bruant's great façade. 195 metres in length, it comprises a projecting central pavilion and two corner pavilions surmounted with monumental war trophies. The form of the bays that articulate the façade varies at each of the four levels, the last being offset

by a cornice. The dormer windows in the roof are decorated with highly fanciful trophies.

The central pavilion, housing the grand salon, opens by means of a passageway onto the royal courtyard. Huge pilasters support an immense arcade. In 1733 the decoration of the façade was entrusted to Guillaume Coustou, the most famous sculptor of his day. The great bas-relief in the tympanum represents Louis XIV on horseback between two seated Virtues, *Justice* and *Prudence*. The plan included another two statues in the round placed on high plinths in front of the twin pilasters of the arcade, *Mars* and

Minerva seated (replaced in 1966 by copies). The same central pavilion opening onto three arcades is to be found on the western and eastern façades of the royal courtyard. The fourth pavilion, which forms the façade of the church of Saint Louis des Invalides (also known as the "Soldiers' Church"), probably designed by Jules Hardouin-Mansart, has a more elaborate outline, the pilasters being replaced by twin columns. Arcades on two levels form a gallery around the circumference of the courtyard: its purpose was originally to enable the pensioners to walk about sheltered from the inclemencies of the weather. Decoration was limited to dormer windows and four sculpted groups in the angles of the courtyard. Each flank of the courtyard contains a suite of two large rooms serving as refectories, the whole capable of receiving 1500 people. They were originally decorated with paintings portraying episodes from the war with the Netherlands (1672-1678). Thus the first pensioners of the hospice had before their eyes the campaigns they had just left. Two of the four refectories have been restored, corresponding today to the Turenne and Henri IV Rooms. The paintings in the present-day François I Room are probably by

Above:
west pediment of the
royal courtyard with
the double sundial
dating from 1770.
© A. Derenne/
La Goëlette.

Top left and right:
statues
of *Strength* and
Justice,
two of the four
figures of the virtues
sculpted by

Coysevax
for the first
storey
of the façade
of the Dome Church.
© A. Derenne/
La Goëlette.

Top centre:
the Dome
Church
from the
south-west.
© C. Bibollet/
Top.

Joseph Parrocel. Already in 1706 their very bad condition had been noted and they were repainted. This group of buildings, of which the foundation stone was laid on 20 November 1671, was completed in 1675, with the exception of a few decorations. To the east of the hospice an infirmary in cruciform plan was added in 1679, and matching it to the west, lodgings for the priests in 1691. Lastly, Jules-Robert de Cotte constructed a wing for the officers in 1749. In this way the institution recovered its original symmetry. In the middle of the 18th century the intendant's garden was again improved with the addition of an ornamental lake in the south-west corner and a bakery in the south-east corner of the square in front of the royal church.

One entered the Soldiers' Church at the far end of the courtyard. The coexistence of this with the "domed church" or "royal church" can be explained by a change of plan and of architect. Whereas the main work on the hospice was completed in 1674, Libéral Bruant had not yet started work on the church. In March 1676, Louvois, then Minister for War, summoned Jules Hardouin-Mansart and asked him for a project. Mansart went back to the nave such as it was in Bruant's project and turned it into the chancel of his new domed church, the two buildings being connected by means of a sanctuary. This difficult linkage was to lead gradually to the individualisation of the two spaces.

In order to assure the smooth running of the institution, the construction of the Soldiers' Church was very rapid. Started in 1676, it was completed in 1678. The organ case was ordered in 1679 and Louis XIV came to hear its registration on 1 March 1682. The nave has nine bays; the arcades lead to aisles that support the galleries. A clerestory gives light to the nave and a barrel vault with lunettes identical to that of the Oratory Church constructed by Jacques Lemercier (1621-1630). In this very sober interior, the decoration consists of pilasters of a composite order, transverse rib arches and the main line

Above:
one of the upper galleries of the royal courtyard.
© A. Derenne/
La Goëlette.

Top:
general view of the royal courtyard.
© C. Rose/
CNMHS-Spadem
1993.

Former Council
chamber,
currently the office of
the Director of the
Army Museum,
paintings by Jules

Varnier portraying
the successive
governors of the
Invalides, 1841.
© A. Derenne/
La Goëlette.

string-course that links them. Two reasons led to the project for the Dome Church: the king's glory - in this hospice which was the great concern of his reign, and "the proprieties". Soldiers could not indeed take the same path as the king. Bruant had imagined the soldiers entering the church from the rear while the king would enter from the courtyard. Mansart turned Bruant's idea on its head: the king would enter from the chapel on the south side. Even so, this way had to be just as splendid, so the architect imagined, in 1702, placing a colonnade and pavilions in front of the dome, forming a square where royal pomp could be displayed. The contract for the foundations was signed in February 1677 but budgetary difficulties slowed down building work on this prestigious edifice. The tambour was completed in 1687, the dome in 1690 and the lantern was in place by 1691. The decorative sculptures and paintings were not completed until 1706. Louis XIV was able to inaugurate his chapel on 22 August 1706.

The plans for the royal church were directly inspired by the project for the Bourbon Chapel in Saint Denis designed by François Mansart, great uncle of Jules Hardouin. One finds several of its traits: passages in the crossing pillars leading to the corner chapels, galleries supported by columns set up against the pillars and the separation of the cupola into two elements. Its layout in the form of a Greek cross inscribed within a square, surmounted with a large cupola over the crossing and flanked by four circular chapels in the corners, can be traced back to Saint Peter's in Rome or indeed to Lemercier's church of the Sorbonne (1635-1642). The iconography, though very coherent, is more original. It is centred on the figure of Saint Louis and the doctors of the church. Louis IX, a distant ancestor of Louis XIV, achieved a union of things sacred with the monarchy. The Fathers of the Church are the guarantors of religious orthodoxy (Louis XIV had revoked the edict of Nantes in 1685). The façade presents several orginal characteristics. The decoration of the portico is offset by the bareness of the lateral walls. The verticals are

reinforced by the superimposed orders and, in the central axis, by the superpositioning of columns - and not of bays. This deliberate wish to create an upward dynamic for the façade - it reaches its highest point at 101 metres - is very evident at the level of the dome, whose elevation is much greater than that of the cupola. Both themes, royal and ecclesiastical, are present in the series of sculptures which were realised from 1690 to 1706. This decoration, which can be seen complete in the engraving published in the *Description historique de l'hôtel royal des Invalides* by the Abbé Pérau in 1756, has almost entirely disappeared. A few sculptures have nonetheless survived: to the right of the portal, *Saint Charlemagne* sculpted by Antoine Coysevox, and to the left, Saint Louis by Nicolas Coustou, as well as the four cardinal Virtues - *Prudence*, *Temperance*, *Justice* and *Strength* - from the original cornice of Coysevox and the hanging trophies in lead on the sides of the dome. The pediment with the arms of France (disfigured during the Revolution) was surmounted with the two figures of *Faith* and *Charity* seated on the inclines and framed by other Virtues. At each corner of the square part a group of two Fathers of the Church had been erected. The attic storey had 16 statues, including the twelve apostles. The façade of the dome, as it is today, thus corresponds neither to the wishes of Hardouin-Mansart, who had enriched it with numerous sculpted copings and

amortizements, nor to the wishes of Louis XIV, who had made of it a veritable religious manifesto.

Inside, Hardouin-Mansart made use of all the axes available in his plan: thus, from each chapel the three others are visible at different angles. The two wings on the transverse axis were themselves designed as chapels, terminating in an apse with half-dome vaults. The cupola is amply lighted by the tambour bays while the calotte receives sunlight from the slanting lunettes that prolong the attic bays, invisible from the inside. The altar is situated in an intermediary oval space, assuring the liturgical link with the Soldiers' Church. The iconographic plan was profoundly modified through the slowness of work and the evolution of the reign. However the most extensive upsets were caused by the Revolution and by the change in the purpose of the church which became, like that of Sainte Geneviève, a "temple of Mars" devoted to great military leaders. Only the painted decorations and the bas-relief sculptures have been entirely preserved. The sculptures in the chapels almost all disappeared during the Revolution. Upon entering, one can find, from left to right, in the chapel of Saint Jerome, a reliquary which once contained a hat of Saint Helen and the sword Napoleon used at Eylau. In a niche is placed the tomb of Jérôme Bonaparte (1862). The chapel of the Virgin (west side) owes its name to

From top to bottom and from left to right: façade of the Dome Church in the 18th century showing all the sculptures in position, engraving. © Musée de l'Armée, Paris.

Cross-section of the Dome Church c. 1730, engraving. © Musée de l'Armée, Paris.

Right-hand page: the interior of the Soldiers' Church (Saint Louis des Invalides), seen from the high altar and the glass window separating the nave from the Dome Church © C. Rose/ CNMHS-Spadem 1993.

the altar surmounted by a statue of the Virgin by Pigalle which once was to be found there. It had been replaced in 1800 by the tomb of Turenne, designed by Le Brun and sculpted by Tuby, originally in the basilica of Saint Denis. The chapel of Saint Gregory contains the tomb of Marshal Lyautey by Albert Laprade, set in place in 1963, and, in an urn deposited in 1928, the heart of La Tour d'Auvergne. The paintings in the chancel are by Noël Coypel: the *Assumption of the Virgin* in the half-dome and the *Holy Trinity* on the vault. The high altar is by Visconti, constructed from 1843 to 1853 on the site of the earlier altar by Bartholomé. The baldachin with wreathed columns on a cavetto is a pastiche of that by Bernini in Saint Peter's, Rome. The chapel of Saint Ambrose houses since 1938 the tomb of Marshal Foch by Paul Landowski. In the chapel of Saint Teresa (east side) can be found the tomb of Vauban by Etex erected in 1846-1847. Lastly, the chapel of Saint Augustin received the tomb of Joseph Napoléon by Crépinet in 1866.

When the cupola was finished in 1690, the initial decoration by Charles de Lafosse on the theme of "the glory of the king" was no longer topical. Pierre Mignard received a commission from Louvois but died in 1695 before he could execute his project. Mansart, who was appointed Superintendent of Buildings in 1699, turned in 1702 to his protégé Lafosse and to Jouvenet, Coypet and Bon Boullogne (who was responsible for the paintings in the chapels of Saint Jerome, Saint Ambrose and Saint Augustin). Above the short cornice runs a frieze with relief medallions (restored under the Restoration) showing twelve kings of France, all of them defenders of the faith: Clovis, Dagobert, Pépin the Short, Charlemagne, Louis the Debonair, Charles the Bald, Philippe-Auguste, Saint Louis, Louis XII, Henri IV, Louis XIII and Louis XIV. The pendentives of the four arcades were decorated by Lafosse with the evangelists. In the lower section, the cupola is divided into twelve compartments figuring the apostles painted by Jouvenet. In the upper section Lafosse has portrayed Saint Louis presenting his crown, sword and coat of arms to Christ.

With the return of Napoleon's ashes, the question was raised as to where they should be definitively interred. A law of 10 June 1840 established the installation of Napoleon's tomb beneath the dome of the Invalides. Louis Visconti, winner of the competition, proposed to excavate the centre of the crossing to install an isolated deep-laid tomb surrounded by a gallery. Work started in 1841 with the destruction of the marble mosaic on the floor. Twelve huge statues by Pradier, symbolising Napoleon's victories, keep watch over the porphyry tomb in which the Emperor has rested since 2 April 1861. After a visit to Napoleon's coffin, deposited in the chapel of Saint Jerome, on 8 May 1841, Victor Hugo confessed himself shocked by the demolition

From left to right and from top to bottom: the interior of the Dome Church seen from the high altar. © A. Derenne/ La Goëlette.
Top:
Charles de Lafosse, *Saint Louis surrounded by musician angels* *presenting his arms to Christ,* sketch for the dome cupola, c. 1692, Ø 200 cm, office of the Director of the Army Museum. © Musée de l'Armée, Paris.
Above:
the baldachin of Louis Visconti (1843-1853): paintings by Noël Coypel on the vault and in the half-dome: *The Holy Trinity and The Assumption of the Virgin.* © C. Rose/ CNMHS-Spadem 1993.

work which then seemed an act of vandalism (in fact the construction of Napoleon's mausoleum continues by many authors to be classed as an act of destruction, like the exactions of the Revolution). The succeeding generation, that of Maurice Barrès, was fascinated by this void: "Fill this crypt, where lies sublimity, with your thoughts; level down history, do away with Napoleon: you are destroying the essence of the century's imagination" (*Les Déracinés*). The transformation of the royal church into an imperial mausoleum reinforced the separation of the two elements of the church as conceived by Mansart, even if Visconti was careful enough to rebuild the altar. The grille which separated them was replaced in 1873 by a marble partition surmounted by a huge window, thus preventing all communication. Lastly, the digging of the crossing, apart from the destruction of the marble pavement, broke the harmony of the place, as Victor Hugo had felt in 1841: "Though this dome be narrow, history is broad. The day will come when Louis XIV's dome will be given back to him and Napoleon will be given his own sepulchre" (*Choses vues*).

Since this last outrage to the Invalides few changes have been made, apart from the inelegant parasitic constructions that caused the façades to be classed as historical monuments in 1935. From this date efforts have been made to restore if not the actual condition, at least the spirit of the building such as it was in the middle of the 18th century. From 1936 onwards the stables along the boulevard de Latour-Maubourg were pulled down, as they hid the officers' quarters. In 1962 a systematic clearance of the surroundings was undertaken, reintegrating the building into Parisian urbanism; the intendant's garden was re-created, and the dome and the façades of the church repointed in 1989. The restoration of the paintings in the cupola is currently proceeding.But it is unlikely that Napoleon's tomb, having become the heart of the Invalides, will one day leave this place.
François Robichon

JE·DESIRE·QUE·MES·CENDRES·REPOSENT
SUR·LES·BORDS·DE·LA·SEINE
AU·MILIEU·DE·CE·PEUPLE·FRANÇAIS
QUE·J'AI·TANT·AIME.

THE ARMY MUSEUM

By placing the martial pomp of his reign, in the form of great pictorial compositions, before the eyes of invalid soldiers, the objects of his solicitude, was not Louis XIV laying the foundations of a memorial? Intended for the lodging and care of his soldiers, the Hôtel des Invalides thus bore the memory of their most recent combats.

When the creation of the Arts Museum entailed the evacution of the grand gallery of the Louvre, it was quite natural that on the orders of Louis XVI, d'Angiviller, in 1776-1777, transfered under military escort the collection of relief plans of French fortresses commenced by Louvois a century earlier. The revolutionary period saw the arrival of the enemy flags removed from the cathedral of Notre-Dame in 1793 for the benefit of the church of Saint Louis des Invalides which had become the Temple of Mars. At the same time as becoming a necropolis, the Hôtel des Invalides continued to receive war trophies during the Revolution and the Empire. The ceremony which on 17 May 1807 marked the handing over to Field-marshal Sérurier, governor of the Invalides, of the

Alphonse de Neuville,
*Defence of the Longboyau gate,
21 October 1870,*
1879,
oil on canvas,
89 x 130 cm.
© Musée
de l'Armée, Paris.

Pierre L'Enfant,
*The Battle
of Fontenoy,
17 May 1745,*
oil on canvas,
250 x 273 cm
(detail).
© Musée
de l'Armée, Paris.

35

sword and insignia of the Prussian king Frederick II, stayed alive in all memories. The sword of Frederick the Great is still to be found in the Army Museum, but 1417 flags and standards were burned on 30 March 1814 when the troops allied against Napoleon (Russia, Austria, Prussia, England) entered Paris. However, other colours came to replace them, and the memorial character of the Hôtel des Invalides was in fact strengthened during the course of the nineteenth century.

It was as it were in the direct line of this evolution that two museums came to be housed in the Invalides. The first, in 1871, was the Artillery Museum, which had a relatively homogeneous collection, built up over a long period and often added to. The second, the Historical Army Museum, established in 1896, still had to be realised. The fusion of the two museums in 1905 gave birth at last to the Army Museum. The double venture of these collections, together with the differences and the complementarity of the missions of these

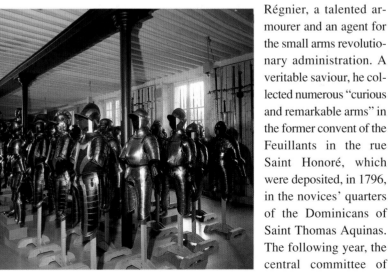

museums, still furnish an explanation of the nature of the Army Museum of today. Whereas the Invalides indisputably owes much to Louvois, the creation of the Artillery Museum was in a certain sense the creation of a relative of the minister. Field-marshal d'Humières, grand master of Artillery from 1685 to 1694 decided to regroup, largely for educational purposes, the royal and regimental arms in the Arsenal. Numerous small scale models of artillery were added, notably those made by Lieutenant-General de Vallière and Inspector of Artillery Gribeauval. Yet the revolutionary period did not not go by without causing destruction. It might even have been fatal to the collection were it not for the zeal of Edme Régnier, a talented armourer and an agent for the small arms revolutionary administration. A veritable saviour, he collected numerous "curious and remarkable arms" in the former convent of the Feuillants in the rue Saint Honoré, which were deposited, in 1796, in the novices' quarters of the Dominicans of Saint Thomas Aquinas. The following year, the central committee of

From left to right and from top to bottom: Henri IV Room, c. 1885. © Musée de l'Armée, Paris.

Turenne Room or Flag Room at the beginning of the century. © Musée de l'Armée, Paris.

The Arsenal in May 1987. © Musée de l'Armée, Paris.

Attributed to Fournier-Sarlovèze, *Crossing the Beresina in 1812*, gouache, 45 x 64 cm. © Musée de l'Armée, Paris.

artillery established the Artillery Museum. Enriched with prizes of war and the expropriated property of émigrés, notably from the Prince of Condé's collection in Chantilly and from the Sedan Gallery, the collections, though carefully maintained, remained nonetheless largely unknown. The romantic period witnessed an upsurge of interest. Although errors proliferate in the illustrated weekly *Le Magasin pittoresque* of 1833, it does have the merit of praising the armour gallery by appealing to the sentiment of national pride. The creation, by Napoleon III, of the museum of sovereigns was to upset this

fine arrangement: royal arms and armours were taken away to be exhibited at the Louvre. In 1872 the Artillery Museum left Saint Thomas Aquinas and came to occupy the ground floor rooms of the west wing of the Invalides. All that Napoleon III had borrowed was returned to the Artillery Museum which then constituted a magnificent contribution to the future Army Museum, including the armours of the Kings of France, the collections of royal arms, arms of war, of hunting and of tournament, oriental arms, and small artillery models. Guided with enthusiasm and marked by the will of some individuals, the

PASSAGE DU PONT D'ARCOLE

For the whole
double page,
photos
© Musée
de l'Armée, Paris.

Crossing the bridge
of Arcole on
15 November 1796,
image d'Epinal
by Pellerin, c. 1860.

Anon, An exempt of
the Maréchaussée
with prisoner, trooper
from the 6th Regiment
of Light Cavalry,
dragoon of the Noailles

Regiment, trooper from
the 6th Regiment of Light
Cavalry according
the ordinance of 1779,
oil on canvas,
51 x 111 cm.

Anon,
Hussars of the
Bercheny,
Chamborant and
Conflans Regiments

according to the
ordinance of 1779,
c. 1779,
oil on canvas,
37 x 72 cm.

realisation of the Army Museum, an essentially patriotic initiative in this period haunted by the revenge of Sedan, is more novel. Its origins go back to the year of the construction of the Eiffel Tower. In the Universal Exhibition of 1889, the pavilion of the War Ministry was erected on the west side of the Invalides esplanade. Souvenirs and portraits of military men, a topographical section with relief plans, uniforms and colours were a very great success as much with amateurs and collectors as with the general public. The steering committeee included General Vanson, the painters Meissonier and Edouard Detaille, Captain Saski. None of them was able to reconcile himself to the temporary nature of this display, which put together objects from numerous private collections, and it was Germain Bapst, the committee secretary, who pointed out that "The history of the Army is a great lesson to all, and each of the exhibits brings, however modestly, something of the totality of France". At first informally gathered around Meissonier (who died in 1891), these men decided to found, in 1893, a society of military history to which they gave the name of "la Sabretache". It was the spearhead of this battle for a museum whose aim was to house "the image and relics of soldiers alongside captured colours on the threshold of the tombs of their Emperors and great captains," (*Carnet de la Sabretache*, 1893). Finally on 31

Anon,
*Esterházy Regiment
and an exempt from
the Maréchausée
with a prisoner,*
*according to the
ordinance of 1779,*
c. 1779,
oil on canvas,
36 x 63 cm.

Anon,
*Dragoons of the
Artois, Orléans,
Dauphin and
Monsieur Regiments*
*according to the
ordinance of 1779,*
c. 1779,
oil on canvas,
50 x 108 cm.

Anon, *Light cavalrymen
of the 4th, 5th and
6th Regiments, French
guard, Swiss guard
and the King's Infantry*
*Regiment, according
to the ordinance
of 1779,* c. 1779,
oil on canvas,
32 x 58 cm.

Anon,
*Hussars of the
Esterházy, Conflans,
Chamborant and
Bercheny Regiments*
*according
to the ordinance
of 1779,* c. 1779,
oil on canvas,
51 x 112 cm.

From left to right and from top to bottom:
Jean Auguste Dominique Ingres, *Napoleon on the imperial throne in ceremonial dress,* c. 1804, oil on canvas, 260 x 163 cm. © Musée de l'Armée, Paris.

The du Quesnoy corridor, with the d'Ornano collections; at the far end *Portrait of Maria Walewska* by François Gérard, 1812. © Musée de l'Armée, Paris.

Antoine Gros, *General Count Antoine de Lasalle (1775-1809) receiving the surrender of the Stettin garrison on 30 October 1806,* 1808, oil on canvas, 300 x 200 cm. © Musée de l'Armée, Paris.

October 1896, Félix Faure, President of France, signed the decree that created the Historical Army Museum which was to be placed under the aegis of the War Ministry and attached to the general staff. Six weeks later General Vanson was appointed the museum's first director. The painter Edouard Detaille, whose finest works were the proud boast of the museum, explained: "This is a museum for national education and it now becomes the sanctuary, the sacred temple, in which historical memories and military relics find a permanent setting, serving as a lesson for the honour of the country and the French army".

Six large rooms were taken over in the west wing. The collections, however, still had to be assembled. Great or small, contributions flowed in, from the caftan of Abdelkader, erstwhile Emir of Algeria, offered by his son, to souvenirs of the field-marshals of the Empire. The Turenne Room, a former refectory for officers, was inaugurated by the President of France on 12 July 1897. It presented, in the neo-imperial showcases one can still see today, the general history of the army, from the sixteenth century down to 1816, a large space being devoted to the revolutionary and imperial periods. Opposite, the Bugeaud Room (today the Vauban Room) was intended to cover the period from 1816 to the Third Republic, showing that the museum was already concerning itself with current events. In his programme of military

history, General Vanson even wished to set up a "repository of models for painters". Soon a specialised library and a print-room were established. Success came very quickly: at the beginning of the century, nearly 160,000 visitors a year were recorded.

The fusion of the two museums in 1905 respected the specific character of each collection. The two churches were at this time attached to the museum, whose director was officially, according to the statutes of the public institution that was later set up, "the guardian of the Emperor's tomb". The task of the new Army Museum, as depositary of an exceptional heritage, was to make it available to the public. This was the motivation for the various museological developments in the course of this century that were the result of the various talents of the civil and military curators. The collections belonging to the Artillery Museum were principally incorporated into the department of Ancient Arms and Armour, to be found on the ground floor of the west wing, which presents the evolution of armaments from Antiquity to the seventeenth century. One can see hunting and court weapons, the royal collections (including those of oriental arms) and the collection of Georges Paulhiac which was acquired in 1968. The number of masterpieces is incalculable, most of them of royal or princely origin; the less prestigious arms have

been assembled in the "arsenal", a veritable reserve to which access is nonetheless possible, and which tries to recreate the atmosphere of arsenals of former times. Such is the wealth of valuable exhibits in this department that it must be placed among the leading armouries in the world, long with the Tower of London, the Waffensammlung in Vienna, the Armería real of Madrid etc. The highly important collection of miniature artillery models has its place in the Gribeauval Room, the first room to be designed with the help of a museum architect (1992). The presence in this wing of two rooms dedicated to the two World Wars is explained by the problem of the allocation of space within the Invalides.

Most of the historical rooms, covering the period from the ancient monarchy to 1871, are grouped in the east wing, which opens onto the astonishing monumental sculpted gateway to the Historical Army Museum (1900). They mingle iconography and an appropriate selection of arms and uniforms evoking the great figures of French military history from Turenne to Bugeaud. These rooms reserve a large space for the Revolution and the Empire, presenting notably outstanding souvenirs of Napoleon and his field-marshals. On the ground floor are the Turenne Room, devoted to colours and standards, and the Vauban Room, housing an evocation of the cavalry from 1800 to 1940 as well as a collection of regular small arms. An historical room dedicated to the Hôtel des Invalides still has to be created. It should

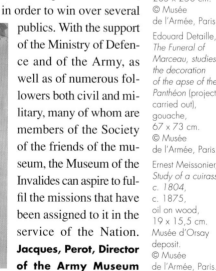

form part of the gradual renovation of the museum that is already under way and which, envisages the restoration of its collections.

On the threshold of the twenty-first century the Army Museum must reaffirm its vocation as a great national museum of military history. Broadening its horizons to the contemporary period, it must also be a witness for the defence of the country. Yet the Army Museum has also proved to be a museum of history - the history of the army being an integral part of the history of the Nation, and a museum of art, by virtue of the works of art in the strict sense that it houses (paintings, drawings or prints) and because of the esthetic qualities of certain objects, such as the arms of Negroli. The Army Museum is also a museum of society, able to reflect the originality of the military community and of its role, and lastly it is a museum of science and technology. As the depositary of an exceptional heritage, the museum must be both a reference for specialists and a place open to the general public, including schoolchildren. It should broaden the scope of its activities, from cinema to music, in order to win over several publics. With the support of the Ministry of Defence and of the Army, as well as of numerous followers both civil and military, many of whom are members of the Society of the friends of the museum, the Museum of the Invalides can aspire to fulfil the missions that have been assigned to it in the service of the Nation. **Jacques, Perot, Director of the Army Museum**

From left to right and from top to bottom: Alphonse de Neuville et Edouard Detaille, *At the bottom of the knapsack, (panorama of the battle of Champigny), 1882,* oil on canvas, 285 x 250 cm. © Musée de l'Armée, Paris.

Edouard Detaille, *The Funeral of Marceau, studies for the decoration of the apse of the Panthéon (project not carried out),* gouache, 67 x 73 cm. © Musée de l'Armée, Paris.

Ernest Meissonier, *Study of a cuirassier,* c. 1804, c. 1875, oil on wood, 19 x 15,5 cm. Musée d'Orsay deposit. © Musée de l'Armée, Paris.

ARMOUR

The masterpieces from the sixteenth century presented here are a reminder of the extreme richness of the ancient collections of the Army Museum.
The armour of the dauphin, the future Henri II, decorated with the princely monogram in silver damascene, was

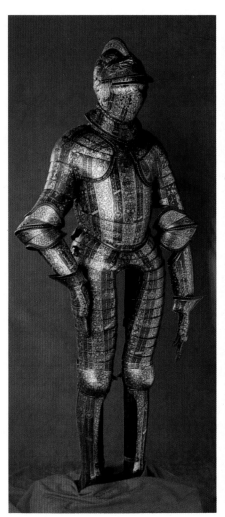

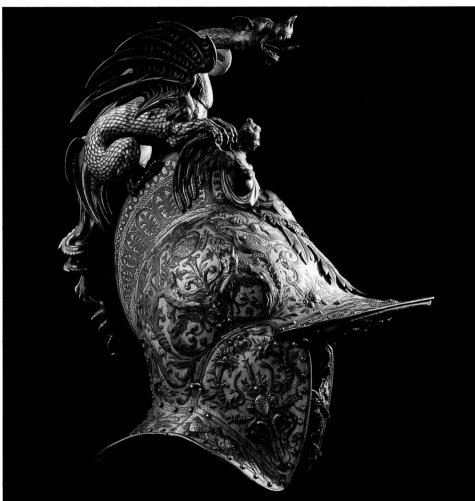

made in 1540 by Fillipo Negroli, a famous Milanese armourer. The steel helmet with griffon, characterised by its strange shapes evoking a dragon's head, was probably made around 1545-1550 by Giovanni Paolo Negroli, another member of the celebrated dynasty of Milanese armourers. The steel helmet with chimera, of probably Flemish workmanship from about 1560-1570, exemplifies the same

Above, from left to right: Filipo Negroli, armour of the Dauphin, the future Henri II, c. 1540, blackened steel damascened with silver, 176 x 75 cm.
Helmet with chimera, Flemish workmanship, c. 1560-1570, embossed, engraved, gilded and damascened iron, 61 x 24 cm.
Opposite: Niccolò Silva, trooper's armour, c. 1510, 183 x 60 cm.
© Musée de l'Armée, Paris.

mannerist taste, as does the embossed working of the fine armour that might have belonged to King Charles IX. This is of French handiwork dating from about 1565/1570. The armour made in about 1510 in the Milanese workshops of Niccolo Silva is

Below, from left to right: Giovanni Paoli Negroli, helmet with griffon, c. 1545-1550, embossed, engraved and gilded iron, 28 x 19 cm.

Armour of Charles IX (?), French workmanship, c. 1565-1570, embossed, engraved and gilded iron, 182 x 65 cm.

Opposite: Wilhelm von Worms the Elder, trooper's armour, c. 1520, iron, 137 x 79 cm.

© Musée de l'Armée, Paris.

also a reminder, in the beauty of its forms and the elegance of its decoration, of the high talents of the Milanese armaoli of the 16th century. By contrast the armour bearing the mark of Wilhelm von Worms the Elder, are a reminder of the work of German armourers at the beginning of the Renaissance, and more particularly in Nuremberg.

Jean-Pierre Rerverseau

HUNTING WEAPONS

The department of Arms
and Armour of the
Army Museum houses a
very important collection
of hunting weapons
as can be seen from the
shoulder weapons
depicted here. Missile and
projectile weapons,
bows and cross-bows
were commonly used for
both war and hunting.
The stone-bow (shooting
little balls of earth),
designed for hunting
small birds, is a reminder
of Catherine de
Medici's predilection for
hunting. The wheel-
lock arquebus with the
stock inlaid with
mother-of-pearl
corresponds to the type of
luxury weapon used
in German lands for big
game hunting.
Of rare sumptuousness,

For the whole
double page,
photos © Musée de
l'Armée, Paris.
From left to right and
from top to bottom:
stone thrower
belonging to

Catherine de Medicis,
French or Florentine
workmanship,
c. 1550, sculpted
wood and
damascened iron
82 x 42 cm. (détail
de l'arbrier).

Wheel-lock
arquebus belonging
to Louis XIII, French
workmanship,
c. 1615-1620,
engraved and chased
iron, sculpted wood,
length 133 cm.

with its sculptured
stock, its engraved
mechanism and fittings,
a wheel-lock
arquebus that belonged
to Louis XIII is
an evocation of the
king's passion for
firearms. From the Munich
School, famed
in the early seventeenth
century for its
handsome arms,
come wheel-lock
arquebuses made by
some of the great
masters: G. Muller,
H. Borstoffer, Master L. D.,
A. Vischer.
Worked in ivory, this pair
of flint pistols
from the Baroque period
seems to be more
an object of
curiosity than a warrior's
accessory.
Jean-Pierre Reverseau

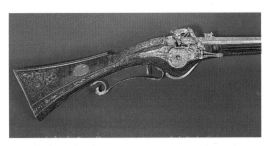

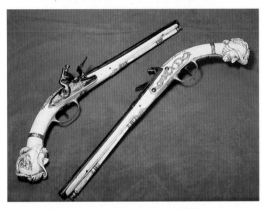

Wheel-lock arquebus, German workmanship, c. 1600, damascened iron, engraved brass, and ebony with horn inlay, length 90 cm.

Johan Louroux, pair of flint-lock pistols, Maastricht, c. 1660-1670, ivory, engraved iron with gold damascene, gilded brass.

Three wheel-lock arquebusses, from the top: G. Müller and H. Bortoffer, c. 1610, engraved and gilded iron, wood with engraved horn inlay, length 125 cm.;

H. Bortoffer, c. 1625-1630, iron and wood with horn inlay, length 125 cm.; Master L.D. and A. Vischer, iron and wood covered with horn inlaid with ivory, length 121 cm.

ORIENTAL ARMS

The turbaned helmet of Sultan Bajazet II is one of the finest pieces in the oriental collections of the Army Museum: this Ottoman head protector from the end of the 15th century is in the form of a bulb enlivened with grooved spirals, burnished all over and bearing a damascened inscription in nakhshî characters: "The imam, courageous master of the victory, Sultan Bayazid,

Armour of Iro Iro Odoshi Domaru No Yoroi type, Japan, end of 16th century, lacquered and gilded steel with polychrome silk, 125 x 45 cm.
© Musée de l'Armée, Paris.

War dress of the Emperor K'ien Long, Manchu China, end of 18th century, embroidered yellow silk, three superimposed tunics, full-dress helmet covered with gold inlay, 224 x 63 cm.
© Musée de l'Armée, Paris.

son of Sultan Mohammed
Khan". From the
Manchu region of China,
towards the end of the
18th century, comes
an exceptional piece, the
war costume of the
Emperor K'ien Long
(1736-1796): full-dress
clothes in yellow
silk embroidered with a
motive representing
a tiger with five claws,
the imperial symbol.
Three tunics were worn
one on top of the
other, the second armed
with blades of gilt steel; a
full-dress helmet
covered with gold inlay
and surmounted with an
aigrette and a pearl
complete the costume. The
art of armoury was
reknowned in Japan as
early as the 7th century
and expanded until
the middle of the
last century. Japanese
armourers created a
flexible defensive armour
consisting of small metal
plates covered with
lacquer and held in place
by silk lace work.
Jean-Pierre Reverseau

ARTILLERY

For the whole double page, photos © Musée de l'Armée, Paris.

Above, from top to bottom: twelve-pounder basinet cannon on its carriage, 17th century, Grand Dauphin series by Heroldt in Nuremberg, 1663, bronze, 1/6 scale.

Small artillery model offered to Louis XIV by the Franche-Comté to commemorate the annexion of this province to France, gun in engraved and gilded bronze on carriage with wheels of fruit tree wood, 1676, 1/4 scale. Photo P. Merat.

Opposite right and right-hand page, below: views of the Gribeauval Room, inaugurated in November 1992, architect: C. Menu. Photos P. Ruault.

Right-hand page from top to bottom: twelve-pounder cannon of 1732 proportions, partially decorated bronze, 1/6 scale. Eight-inch howitzer of 1743 type, emblazoned and decorated, molten bronze by Jean Maritz, foundry commissioner of the French artillery, 1/4 scale. Photo P. Merat.

Begun almost two centuries ago, at the same time that the Artillery Museum was founded, and constantly enriched ever since by donations, acquisitions and the production of new items, the collection of small models in the Army Museum comprises today almost a thousand pieces. It is one of the richest collections of its kind in the world. Especially remarkable for the variety of its small models, this collection presents all the pieces actually used in the practical application of artillery: canon, swivel guns, mortars, howitzers, mounts.

Created out of the conjunction of art and technology the small models illustrate the extreme skill of the casters who, mastering different techniques such as the delicate moulding of bronze, fine tooling, engraving, sculpture and decorative gilding, produced real masterpieces. This collection, covering an unparalleled span both as regards time and geography, presents three centuries in the history of artillery from the start of the seventeenth century up to the present day.
Sylvie Leluc

COLOURS

"farewell flag of Fontainebleau" because it is the one embraced by Napoleon at the time of his first abdication. Beside the retrospective of national colours and standards, the department looks after the trophies won by France from its enemies. Most of them hang from the vault of the church of Saint Louis des Invalides.
Jean de Lasalle

Held sacred by armies all over the world, the national flag occupies a privileged place in all military museums. More than any other, the Army Museum respects this tradition. It devotes an entire room, the Turenne Room, to displaying the colours and standards of the French army. Alongside this general exhibition, numerous flags and standards are presented amid souvenirs of their epoque because of the special role they had to play in them. The oldest flag on show is that of the contingent of the Grisons, dating from 1619. Following it there are only a few flags from the Ancien Régime as the government of the Republic collected and burned all the flags of the king's armies on 13 August 1793 in the Place de la Grève in Paris. One of the most prestigious flags is that of the 1st Regiment of Foot Grenadiers of the Imperial Guard, better known as the

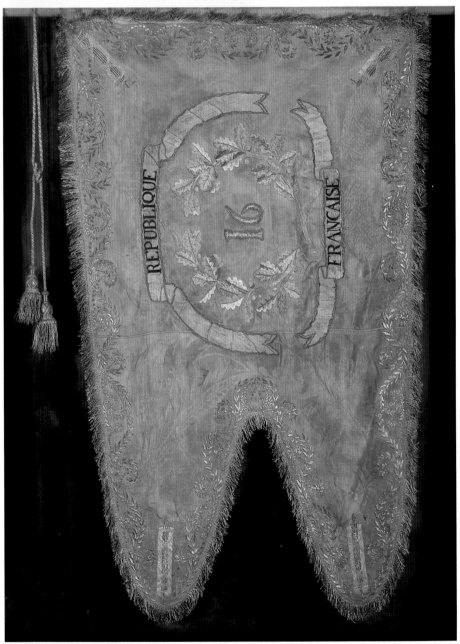

For the whole double page, photos © Musée de l'Armée, Paris. Above, from top to bottom: flag of the 192th Infantry Regiment 1794-1804, obverse. Guidon of the 4th Squadron of the 16th Regiment of Dragoons, 1793, reverse.

Above, from top to bottom: standard of the 2nd Dragoons, reverse.

Hussar standards, 1793-1803, obverse.

UNIFORMS

A uniform is the symbol par excellence of military function. Cursorily described in the 16th century, precisely regulated a century later, illustrated by an often highly faithful iconography, exemplified by an abundant collection of clothing, the uniform is present in all the rooms of the Army Museum, from the ancient monarchy to the present

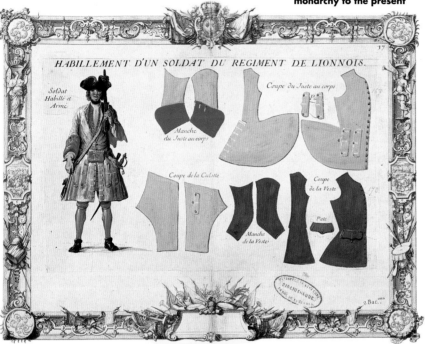

day. At first copied from civilian models, the uniform came to adapt itself to military needs. This evolution, that took place throughout the 18th and 19th centuries, was a perpetual compromise between the quest for uniformity and the desire to develop esprit de corps, which multiplies the distinctions running against this uniformity. There results a gigantic kaleidoscope in

which forms and colours are infinitely varied, from the most humble dress to the most sumptuous of costumes, from the 18th century to the end of the second Empire. After 1870, the uniform became less ostentatious and the soldier of the Belle Epoque is the last of a highly colourful series. Trench warfare imposed horizon blue

cloth, becoming khaki between the world wars. Throughout the rooms of the museum, emblematic figures, mannequins in uniforms that though sometimes faded are steeped in history, seem to wink at the visitor: Fanfan-la-Tulipe, the soldier of Napoleon's Old Guard, the Zouave from the Alma, the infantryman from the Marne and so many others! Jacques de Varax

suisses et autres régiments, manuscript T.I, 21 x 35 cm.
Carle Vernet, Field-marshal of the Empire in court dress, 1812, gouache from Colonel Bardin, règlement sur l'habillement et l'armement des troupes françaises de terre, 1812, manuscript T. IV, pl. 1, 30.5 x 28.5 cm.
Anon, Dragoons

from the Lorraine, Custine, La Rochefoucauld, Jarnac Regiments, according to the ordinance of 1779, c. 1779, oil on canvas, 50 x 109 cm.
Corporal of Grenadier Infantry of the Swiss Regiment of Courten, in French service, 1767.
Infantry officer of the Neustria Regiment, 1780.

MEMORIES OF NAPOLEON

Objects that belonged to Napoleon are presented in the first floor rooms of the east wing of the Army Museum. In the La Fayette Room a table and two chairs are an evocation of the beginnings of Bonaparte's career when he was lieutenant of artillery at Auxonne. In the Egypt Room the sabre and the field glasses used at the battle of the Pyramids and three Mameluke saddles are souvenirs of that campaign. A sword, two sabres, the major general's uniform worn at the **battle of Marengo and a hat are presented in the Consulate Room. The Boulogne Room is devoted exclusively to the memory of the Emperor: the coronation stool, the sword of Austerlitz, the collar of the Légion d'honneur, the grey frock coat, some hats and a reconstruction of a field tent with its furnishings are the most striking exhibits. The horse Vizir is on display in the Eylau Room and in the Montmirail Room a painting by Delaroche shows Napoleon I shortly before his first abdication**

For the whole double page, photos © Musée de l'Armée, Paris. Above: Martin-Guillaume Biennais, collar of the Légion d'honneur belonging to Napoleon I, gold and enamel, 40 x 51 cm.

Left, centre: major general's costume worn by General Bonaparte at the battle of Marengo (14 June 1800), blue cloth, purl braids, height 115 cm.

Left, below: the Emperor's coronation saddle for 2 December 1804, silk velvet, red leather, gold thread embroidery, 67 x 92 x 63 cm.

in 1814. The reconstruction of the bedroom in Longwood House presents the furniture and clothes used on the island of Saint Helena. Opposite, the death mask made from Antommarchi's cast and a display case with various objects worn at the end of his life afford a last vision of this sovereign and war leader. Finally, in the Bugeaud Room, a glass case is devoted to the return of the ashes.
Gérard-Jean Chaduc

Right, above: sabre worn by General Bonaparte at the battle of the Pyramids, steel, ivory, gilded copper, wood, velvet, length 82 cm. Deposit of the Musée du Louvre, Paris.

Right, centre: Paul Delaroche, *Napoleon I at Fontainebleau at the time of his abdication in 1814*, oil on canvas, 177 x 131 cm.

Opposite, left: reconstruction of Napoleon's drawing-room in Longwood House on Saint Helena, steel folding bed by Desouches in which the Emperor died on 5 May 1821.

RECENT CONFLICTS

The main part
of the collections of the
department of
contemporary military
history - from 1871
to the present day - in the
Army Museum, is for
the moment in reserve for
lack of display space.
That part of it relating to
the two World Wars
has been taken
out to make up the 1914-
1918 Room and
the 1939-1945 Room.
These have been
separated by the so-called
"Field-marshals'
landing", for personal
objects belonging

For the whole
double page,
photos © Musée de
l'Armée, Paris.
Above,
from left to right:
Georges Scott,
*Portrait
of Field-marshal
Foch on*

horseback,
1930,
oil on canvas,
125 x 91.5 cm.
Félix Valloton,
Verdun, 1917,
oil on canvas,
115 x 146 cm.
© Musée
de l'Armée, Paris.

Above,
from left to right:
soldier from
the 27th Infantry
Regiment,
1914.

Soldier from the
60th Infantry

Regiment, 1916-
1917.

Trooper from the
temporary regiment
of Moroccan
Spahis, 1918.

Moroccan gourmier,
1939-1945.

to field-marshals from both world wars are on display here in individualised cabinets. The 1914-1918 Room was restored in 1988 for the 70th anniversary of the victory. It recounts the history of World War I on all fronts, in a three-part presentation corresponding to the three phases of the war on the western front. The 1939-1945 Room, whose highly documentary museum presentation dates back to the 1960's will be remodelled and reconstituted for the 50th anniversary of the Liberation. In touch with current affairs, the department keeps a display cabinet in the west staircase for conflicts still in progress.
Raymond Noulens

A TOUS LES FRANÇAIS

La France a perdu une bataille!
Mais la France n'a pas perdu la guerre!

Des gouvernants de rencontre ont pu capituler, cédant à la panique, oubliant l'honneur, livrant le pays à la servitude. Cependant, rien n'est perdu!

Rien n'est perdu, parce que cette guerre est une guerre mondiale. Dans l'univers libre, des forces immenses n'ont pas encore donné. Un jour, ces forces écraseront l'ennemi. Il faut que la France, ce jour-là, soit présente à la victoire. Alors, elle retrouvera sa liberté et sa grandeur. Tel est mon but, mon seul but!

Voilà pourquoi je convie tous les Français, où qu'ils se trouvent, à s'unir à moi dans l'action, dans le sacrifice et dans l'espérance.

Notre patrie est en péril de mort.
Luttons tous pour la sauver!

VIVE LA FRANCE !

C. de Gaulle.

GÉNÉRAL DE GAULLE

QUARTIER-GÉNÉRAL,
4, CARLTON GARDENS,
LONDON, S.W.1.

Above, from top to bottom:
Albert Brenet, *French aviators, sailors and infantrymen on leave at the Gare de l'Est in 1939*, gouache, 43 x 80 cm.
Poster of the Appeal of 18 June 1940.

THE MUSEUM
OF RELIEF PLANS

 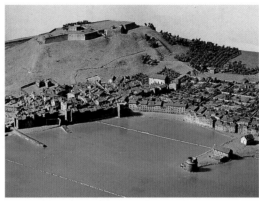 

The installation of the royal collection of relief plans under the timbers of the Hôtel des Invalides dates from 1777. It was moved in that year from the great gallery of the Louvre to make way for the future picture gallery. At first only a small number of privileged people, in possession of the king's authorisation, had access to the gallery with the relief plans. Under the Empire it was opened to the general public in 1810. The museum of relief plans has the distinction therefore of being the oldest of the museums housed within the Hôtel des Invalides. This somewhat obsolete and often misunderstood term of relief plans refers to a unique collection of scale model fortified towns started in 1668 by the Marquis de Louvois, minister under Louis XIV.

The history of the collection is linked to the history of wars of conquest and of national defence, so it is not surprising that towns situated on either side of the current frontiers (Strasburg, Namur) or along the coast (Belle-Île, Brest) are especially well represented. One will also find scale models of towns in former French possessions (Constantine, Corfou) and of various places associated with military expeditions (Rome, Sebastopol).

One of the particularities of the history of this museum is that from the end of the eighteenth century the scale models have been made and restored within the precincts of the gallery itself, which was thus responsible for the creation of its

For the whole double page with relief plans, photos © Musée de l'Armée, Paris. Above, from left to right: the citadel of Saint Nicolas, Marseilles, 1684, 142 x 13 cm., 1/183 scale (detail). Photo C. Carlet.

The port of Saint Tropez, 1716, 155 x 137 cm., 1/600 scale (detail). Photo C. Carlet.

Port and citadel of Belle-Île by Tessier de Derville, king's engineer, 1704; 250 x 230 cm., 1/600 scale (detail). Photo C. Carlet.

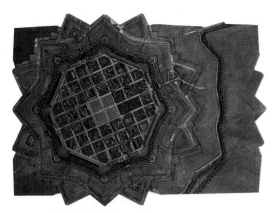

own objects. Production techniques have changed little: the frame is in wood, as are all the buildings. The whole is covered with engraved paper. Vegetation is made with flocked silk or twisted wire.

If the 1/600 scale models as a whole may be considered the brightest ornament of the museum, the latter is not limited to the hundred or so relief plans. The museum collections also include several groups of scale models, such as theoretical models of fortifications constructed in the eighteenth and nineteenth centuries, and geographic relief maps.

Max Polonovski

Above: citadel of Neuf-Brisach, 1706, 447 x 233 cm., 1/600 scale, vertical view of table 1 (detail). Photo C. Carlet.

Centre and below: views of the town of Besançon by Ladevèze, king's engineer, 1722, 621 x 430 cm., 1/600 scale (detail). Photo C. Carlet.

THE MUSEUM OF THE ORDER OF THE LIBERATION

JUREZ DE NE
DEPOSER LES ARMES
QUE LORSQUE NOS
COULEURS, NOS
BELLES COULEURS
FLOTTERONT SUR
LA CATHEDRALE
DE
STRASBOURG.
LECLERC
1er MARS 1941.

For the whole
double page, photos
© Musée de l'Ordre
de la Libération.
Above, from left to
right: plaque
bearing the Koufra
oath.

Radio transmitter
used by the
Resistance.

Plaque from the fort
at Bir-Hakeim.

On 16 November 1940, General De Gaulle created the Order of the Liberation. He defined the scope of its attribution as being "for exceptional actions" and the decoration's ribbon, black for mourning and green for hope, succinctly summed up his vision of France. 1036 crosses were awarded to civilians and military personnel up until 23 January 1946, when this very high distinction ceased to be conferred. Among the recipients 238 were named posthumously, and 105 who were already Companions of the Liberation, lost their lives for France. The order, "this exceptional order of chivalry, created in the darkest hour in the history of France, which kept faith with itself, conjoined in sacrifice and in struggle", will die out with the passing of the last companion. An empty place awaits him in the crypt of Mont Valérien, the shrine of the Resistance.

Adequate expression can never be given to the sum of abnegation and sacrifice that was necessary to lead our country into the victors' camp. Our museum is the guarantor of this memory. Thanks to the initiative of Claude Hettier de Boislambert, Chancellor of the Order, a vast campaign aimed at the companions, their families, holders of Resistance and Free French medals was set up to increase the funds. It is therefore thanks to the devotion of all that the

museum can today present 220 display cabinets throughout three galleries and six rooms. The companions , holders of the Resistance medal, the Free French, members of the Resistance as well as deportees are remembered here, gathered around their leader, General De Gaulle.

This museum is a lesson in history, and bears witness to the greatness of France. The flags burnt in the flames of battle, the clandestine tracts and radio transmitters, sand from Bir-Hakeim, the pitiful cast-off clothing from the deportation camps, the insignia and colours captured from the enemy, the uniforms of the companions of the order, war trophies won in the course of five years of hard fighting - these constitute a moving pilgrimage for the visitor as he moves round the museum. **Jean Simon**

From top to bottom: display cabinet with the collar of the Grand Master of the Order of the Liberation, and the mansucript text of the Appeal of 18 June.

Collar of the Grand Master of the Order of the Liberation.

Cross of the Order of the Liberation.

Façade of the museum of the Order of the Liberation.

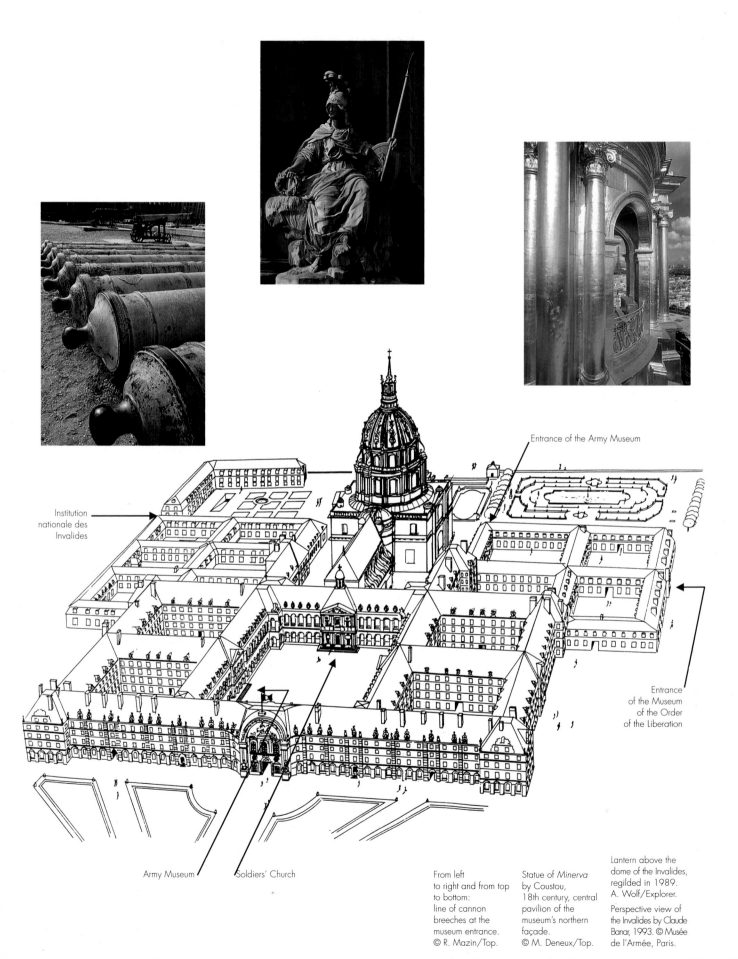

Entrance of the Army Museum

Institution
nationale des
Invalides

Entrance
of the Museum
of the Order
of the Liberation

Army Museum

Soldiers' Church

From left
to right and from top
to bottom:
line of cannon
breeches at the
museum entrance.
© R. Mazin/Top.

Statue of *Minerva*
by Coustou,
18th century, central
pavilion of the
museum's northern
façade.
© M. Deneux/Top.

Lantern above the
dome of the Invalides,
regilded in 1989.
A. Wolf/Explorer.

Perspective view of
the Invalides by Claude
Banar, 1993. © Musée
de l'Armée, Paris.

ICAL INFORMATION

Army Museum
Hôtel national des Invalides 75007 Paris.
Tel. 44 42 37 72.
Open every day (except 1 January, 1
May, 1 November, 25 December)
from 10 a.m. to 5 p.m. (1 October to 31
March); from 10 a.m. to 6 p.m.
(1 April to 30 September).
The Dome Church stays open until 7 p.m.
from 1 June to 31 August.
The entry ticket is valid for
the Army Museum, the Dome Church
with Napoleon's tomb and the

Museum of Relief Plans
tel. 45 51 95 05. Admission to the
corridors, galleries, and Soldiers'
Church is free during normal opening
hours. The ticket offices are to
be found on the left-hand side of the main
courtyard and to the left of the
Dome Church.
• Guided visits and lectures: reception
bureau of the Army Museum,
tel.: 44 42 37 72.
Caisse nationale des Monuments
historiques et des Sites, tel. 44 61 21 67.
• Cinema: exclusive full-length films
shown on afternoons; programme
changes every Wednesday. Morning
showings on demand for associations and
school groups. Tel.: 44 42 37 70.
• Library and documentation centre:
50,000 volumes, 10,000 manuscripts and
autographs, 100,000 prints.
200 French and foreign periodicals
dealing with military history.
Admission restricted to members of the
Society of the Friends of the Army
Museum and to authorised researchers.
Tel.: 44 42 38 38.
• Photothèque: takes orders for all
photographic work. Tel.: 44 42 54 75.

Society of the Friends of the Army Museum
Conferences, visits, magazine :
tel. 44 42 38 38.

Museum of the Order of the Liberation
54 bis, boulevard de Latour-Maubourg,
tel. 47 05 35 15. Open every day from 2
to 5 p.m., except Sundays and holidays.

Museum of Contemporary History
Entrance to the left of the main courtyard,
at the far end. Tel. 44 42 54 91.
Open for the duration of the exhibitions.
This museum, set up in 1914,
belongs to the Ministry of National
Education. It is the only general museum
in France devoted to the whole of 20th
century history. It houses international
collections of a political, social
and cultural nature. 1,500,000 items and
documents from 1870 to the present day
(paintings, posters, photographs,
post cards etc.) deal with the main topics
of French and foreign history
in a series of temporary exhibitions.

For further reading
• [Various], les Invalides. Trois siècles
d'histoire, Paris, Musée de l'Armée,
1974.
• Anne Muratori-Philip,
les Grandes Heures des Invalides,
Paris, Perrin, 1989.
• Bertrand Jestaz, l'Hôtel et l'église des
Invalides, Paris, Picard/CNMHS, 1990.
• Jean-Marcel Humbert, Napoléon aux
Invalides. 1840, le Retour des cendres,
Paris, musée de l'Armée/Fondation
Napoléon/ Ed. de l'Abbaron, 1990.
• Anne Muratori-Philip,
l'Hôtel des Invalides,
Paris, Ed. Complexe/CNMHS, 1992.

Les hors-série Beaux Arts magazine
sont édités par Beaux Arts SA.

Président-Directeur général :
Charles-Henri Flammarion.
Directeur de la publication :
Jean-Christophe Delpierre.
Rédacteur en chef :
Fabrice Bousteau.
Rédactrice en chef adjointe :
Caroline Lesage.
Maquette :
Claire Luxey,
sur un concept de Ruedi Baur.
Secrétariat de rédaction :
Isabelle Arson.
Version anglaise :
Jeremy Drake.

Création et fabrication :
directeur : Alain Alliez,
assisté de Marie-France Wolfsperger.
Marketing :
Isabelle Canals-Noël.
Tél. : 01 56 54 12 35.
Fax : 01 45 38 30 61.
Beaux Arts magazine,
tour Montparnasse,
33, avenue du Maine,
75755 Paris, cedex 15.
Tél. : 01 56 54 12 34.
Fax : 01 45 38 30 01.
RCS Paris B 404 332 942.
Commission paritaire 65094.
ISSN : 0757-2271.
Dépôt légal : décembre 98.
Impression : Mariogros, Turin, Italie.

We would like to thank Jacques Perrot,
Director of the Army Museum,
his office, all the curators and
Anne Pavard for the help they provided
in the preparation of this number.